P9-DDR-170

Bad Blood

Sue Leather

Series Editor: Rob Waring

HEINLE
CENGAGE Learning™

Australia • Brazil • Japan • Korea • Mexico • Singapore • Spain • United Kingdom • United States

HEINLE
CENGAGE Learning

Page Turners Reading Library

Bad Blood
Sue Leather

Publisher: Andrew Robinson

Executive Editor: Sean Bermingham

Senior Development Editor:
Derek Mackrell

Assistant Editors:
Claire Tan, Sarah Tan

Story Editor: Julian Thomlinson

Series Development Editor:
Sue Leather

Director of Global Marketing:
Ian Martin

Content Project Manager:
Tan Jin Hock

Print Buyer:
Susan Spencer

Layout Design and Illustrations:
Redbean Design Pte Ltd

Cover Illustration: Eric Foenander

Photo Credits:
89 Zhu Difeng/Shutterstock,
91 (clockwise from left)
Christophe Testi/Shutterstock,
Jose Gil/Shutterstock,
Randy Miramontez/Shutterstock,
Shutterstock,
92 Santiago Cornejo/Shutterstock

For permission to use material from this text or product, submit all requests online at **www.cengage.com/permissions**
Further permissions questions can be emailed to **permissionrequest@cengage.com**

ISBN-13: 978-1-4240-1839-0

ISBN-10: 1-4240-1839-0

Heinle
20 Channel Center Street
Boston, Massachusetts 02210
USA

Cengage Learning is a leading provider of customized learning solutions with office locations around the globe, including Singapore, the United Kingdom, Australia, Mexico, Brazil, and Japan. Locate your local office at:
international.cengage.com/region

Cengage Learning products are represented in Canada by Nelson Education, Ltd.

Visit Heinle online at **elt.heinle.com**

Visit our corporate website at **www.cengage.com**

Printed in the United States of America
2 3 4 5 6 7 – 14 13 12 11

Contents

Secrets are made to be found out with time.

Charles Sanford

People in the story

Jay Kwan
a private investigator
in San Francisco

Louie Kwan
owner of The Golden Duck
restaurant, Jay's father

Amy Trent
Jay's assistant

Tony Lee
a chef at The Golden Duck
restaurant

Harry Wu
a San Francisco criminal

Bernard Lom
Owner of the Jade Harbor
Restaurant

The story is set in San Francisco, in the USA.

Chapter 1

A telephone call

It started on a Monday morning.

It was nine thirty and Jay Kwan was in his office in Chinatown with his assistant Amy Trent. They were drinking coffee, still getting into the week. Jay took a pen and opened his appointment book to that day's page: Monday, October 20. There was nothing on the page so far.

"What's new?" Jay asked Amy.

"Take a look at these," said Amy as she passed him some new case papers she'd prepared. Amy Trent was new to Jay's office. She had started just a month ago, but Jay liked her already. She was quick, smart, and it looked as though she could be a good investigator. Jay's private investigation business was getting busy and he needed someone good.

Jay took a drink of his coffee and read the new cases for a few moments. They were the usual kind of thing: another missing person, a husband who was seeing another woman. Kwan's Investigation Agency was new, but business wasn't bad. He put the papers down and looked out of the third floor window. From his desk, he could see Stockton Street below. They called San Francisco the "cool gray city," a good name, Jay thought. It was October, fall already, and there were leaves all over the sidewalks. It was foggy and cold and the people at the street markets were wearing heavy coats. Though Jay loved San Francisco, it wasn't his favorite time of year in the city, and it was a particularly hard season for a private investigator.

Like most investigators, Jay did seventy percent of his job on the street. Most people thought it was all done at a desk these days, but that wasn't true. Though there was some desk work, there was still a lot of work to do out of the office. Most days he spent on the street, watching someone, looking for someone.

Suddenly, the telephone rang. Jay picked it up.

"Kwan's Investigation Agency," he answered.

"Jay," said the voice. "It's Ken Fong here . . ."

"Mr. Fong!" Jay was surprised to hear his father's old friend.

"Jay . . . ," said Ken Fong seriously, "it's your father . . ."

"What? Is he OK?"

"Yes, he's OK," said Ken Fong, "but there was a fire at the restaurant last night."

Jay listened for some minutes, then said, "Thanks, Mr. Fong. I'll go and see him immediately."

Jay put the telephone down. Amy looked at him. Jay didn't say anything but jumped up and walked toward the door.

"What is it?" asked Amy.

"Oh nothing . . . I'll tell you later. That was Ken Fong, a friend of my father. I have to go and see my father right now."

Jay took his coat and ran down the stairs to the cold street, wondering what he was going to find. Would his father even talk to him? He ran down Stockton Street all the way to The Golden Duck, his father's restaurant, on Grant Avenue.

Chapter 2

In the kitchen

It had been a whole year, thought Jay, as he ran toward his father's restaurant. Louie Kwan was getting old now; he wanted to retire soon and he wanted his son, Jay, to manage The Golden Duck. Jay wasn't interested in being a restaurant manager. They'd had a big fight about it, and it was a year since they had spoken to each other.

Jay arrived in the alley behind The Golden Duck and looked through the kitchen window. His father was there, preparing the vegetables for lunch as he always did. Louie Kwan didn't see his son. The old man held the large knife and cut the vegetables into thin pieces. Jay grew up watching his father do this. Now it gave him a sad feeling as he watched Louie. He loved him, but it was always so hard to talk to him. Jay took a deep breath. Then he opened the kitchen door and walked in.

"Jay," his father said, smiling. Then he seemed to remember what had happened a year ago, and his face became serious. "What do you want?"

"Father, I umm . . . Ken Fong told me what happened," said Jay. "He said there was a fire here last night."

His father carried on cutting the vegetables. The older man still didn't smile. "Ken!" he said. "It's not his business; he's so stupid."

"He was just being a good friend to you, Father," Jay answered.

"The fire damage is just there in the corner," his father said in a businesslike way. "But it's not too bad. I will have it repaired later. It's nothing to worry about."

Jay looked over at the corner of the kitchen; there was fire damage to the walls. The walls and the ceiling were black, and one of the old wooden tables in the corner had been completely destroyed. It seemed, though, that the fire hadn't caused any real damage to the building.

"Was it an accident?" asked Jay.

Louie Kwan looked away.

"Father?"

"There's this note, too," said Louie. He put his hand in the pocket of his chef's pants and gave Jay a small piece of paper, torn off at the bottom. Jay unfolded the note and read it.

"This is just the beginning," said the handwritten note. "I know."

"What does that mean?" said Jay.

"I don't know what it means," said Louie.

"I know," Jay repeated. "It must mean something."

Louie looked away. "It could mean anything . . . ," he said. "Nothing probably . . ."

"Ken Fong said you didn't want to involve the police," Jay said.

"No, I don't," said Louie. "Well, they came last night; one of the neighbors told them, I guess. I told them it was an accident, hot oil from the wok." Louie pointed at the wok, the big Chinese pan, on top of the stove. "I didn't tell them about the note. I don't want the police involved in this; it's bad for business, bad for everything." Louie's voice was loud; he was getting angry now.

Jay looked at his father. Had someone warned Louie not to tell the police, he wondered? It was hard to say. His father was like a closed book sometimes. Anyway, Jay decided, it was for the best not to involve the police yet.

"I can investigate this, Father," said Jay carefully. "Find out who did it."

"No!" Louie said loudly. He didn't look at Jay.

"The best way you can help me is here at the restaurant," Louie continued in a lower voice.

Jay sighed. The last time he and his father had spoken was just before Jay opened his new investigation agency. Louie had been very angry with his son. Now Jay saw that nothing much had changed.

Louie shook his head. Then he said, "Food! People love to eat. It's the thing that everyone really likes. If you make food, you always make money in Chinatown."

Louie cut the vegetables quickly into small pieces. Louie was a very good chef. In fact, he was one of the best chefs in San Francisco. His restaurant was famous. "The best Chinese food in the west," the *San Francisco Chronicle* said.

"Father . . ."

"Food is part of this family, Jay," his father went on. Now he cut the meat into small pieces. "My grandfather, my father—your grandfather. They were all great cooks, great chefs. Food, food, food, that's what the Kwans do." He pointed his finger at the big old photograph of his father, Winston Kwan, on the opposite wall. The photograph had been there since before Jay was born. Jay looked up at the face of his grandfather, taken when he was in his seventies. It seemed that the serious old man with the little gray beard was looking straight at Jay. Jay looked away.

Jay wanted to be the first Kwan who didn't make rice and vegetables, and his father couldn't really understand it. The twelve months hadn't changed that, he thought. He knew what was coming next: "They don't become private investigators!" thought Jay.

"They don't become private investigators," his father said. He cut the vegetables quickly. There was silence for a minute or two. Then he took the wok and put it onto the huge stove.

Jay stared down at his shoes and said nothing. It was a long time since he and his father had spoken, but the subject was still the same. It was always the same, thought Jay.

"Am I asking too much?!" Louie continued. "Isn't it right for a man to leave his life's work to his only son?"

Jay felt his face get hot as he fought to control his temper. "And isn't it right for a man to make his own way in life?" he said angrily.

There was silence for a few seconds. Louie looked at the wok, not at his son.

Jay took a deep breath. Then he continued, "Look, I didn't come here to argue with you."

Jay knew that this was something that he and his father could never agree on. Both of them were stubborn; neither of them changed their opinions easily. He didn't want to cover the same ground, have the same fight.

"Family is family, Jay." His father went on, "Blood is blood."

It wasn't the first time he'd heard his father say that, and Jay knew that he really believed it. He also knew that his father was a proud man and that he would never ask his son directly for help. But that didn't mean that he didn't need it, Jay told himself. "I'm going to find out who did this," he thought.

Louie threw the vegetables and meat into the hot wok. They made a lot of noise, and suddenly the kitchen was filled with a delicious smell.

"Don't get involved in this," Louie warned his son.

Jay opened the door of the kitchen and turned back toward his father. He wanted to say something, but he didn't know what to say. He left The Golden Duck and walked quickly past the shops on Grant Avenue.

Yes, he thought as he felt the note in his coat pocket, his father was a difficult man.

Chapter 3

Bernard Lom

Jay opened the door of his office. Amy looked at him; she looked as if she wanted to ask him a question.

"Come on," he said to her. "I need you to do some things. I'll tell you as we go."

The small, dark-haired young woman picked up her coat and followed him.

"Someone set fire to my father's restaurant," said Jay as they walked out of the office. "He's OK, though," he added.

"What? But why?" asked Amy as they ran down the stairs. Jay always insisted on running up and down the stairs. He liked to keep fit, and this was one way of doing it. She ran quickly to keep up with him.

"I mean," she said, breathing hard, "why set it on fire, but not burn down the whole restaurant?"

Jay took the note out of his pocket. "It looks like it's a warning of worse things to come," he said. "It says something about it being just the beginning." He showed it to Amy.

"I know," she read, thoughtfully. "What does that mean?"

"I have no idea," said Jay, shaking his head.

"So your father wants you to find out who did it?" she asked.

"No," he answered. "No, he doesn't. He doesn't want me to be a detective at all. My father still thinks I should manage the restaurant, like him."

They stopped at the bottom of the stairs. There was silence for a moment. Amy was still breathing hard; she wasn't quite as fit as Jay yet. Then she said, "Well that's impossible. You have to be you."

"Well, yes, but it's not so easy when you're the only son," Jay replied.

"Or daughter . . ." said Amy.

They walked through to the parking lot under the building.

Jay looked at her. "Anyway, whether my father wants me to do it or not," he said, "I have to find out."

He added, "There's only one person who would want to really hurt my father. And that's Bernard Lom. I'll start with him."

"Bernard Lom? Who's he?"

"The owner of the Jade Harbor restaurant," said Jay. The Jade Harbor was a famous restaurant on the Embarcadero.

"Lom and my father always hated each other," Jay went on. "But about a year ago Lom said that my father had stolen one of his most famous recipes, and there was a big fight between them."

"A recipe?" asked Amy.

"Yes," Jay answered, "for fish."

"They had a fight about fish?" said Amy, amazed.

"That's the way it is with these chefs," said Jay. "They're crazy." He smiled weakly. "But it was a serious matter. Lom said that he wanted to go to a lawyer; you know, to get money from my father for stealing his recipe," said Jay. "But in the end he didn't. I don't know why. He just went away."

"Or not . . ." said Amy. Then she added, "Shall I get someone to watch your father's restaurant?"

"Yes," said Jay. "But first take this note and go and get Sonny to do his thing with it." Sonny was Sonny Lo, the handwriting expert. He was one of those guys who could look at a piece of writing and tell you what kind of person had written it. Jay thought that it wasn't really a science, but he had to admit that it was sometimes useful.

"Oh," Jay went on, "and someone to watch The Golden Duck . . ."

"I can get the security people we had for the Johnson case," said Amy, walking toward her car.

"Yes, good. Jack Burton will give me a good price," said Jay. Jay and Jack Burton were old college friends, and they often helped each other.

"But remember," Jay added, "my father doesn't even want me to do this, so I don't want him to see big security guards all around the place."

"OK, no problem," said Amy. "I'll talk to them about it."

"We'll meet back here later," said Jay, turning to get into his black sports car.

Jay drove out of the parking lot and wondered if Bernard Lom still had a reason to hate Louie Kwan.

Chapter 4

Meetings

Chinatown was as busy as ever as Jay drove through it toward the Embarcadero. He stopped the car, took out his cell phone and called the Jade Harbor restaurant.

Twenty minutes later Jay was talking to Bernard Lom at his restaurant on the waterfront.

"I was very angry with your father," said Lom. "A man's recipe is his recipe."

"He didn't steal your recipe," said Jay calmly.

"Mmm," said Lom. He played with the huge gold ring on his finger and said, "Well, it's all in the past. And the thing is . . . in the end my restaurant is successful." Lom was a short round man with a round face. He waved his hand toward the walls. "I mean, look around," he said.

Jay looked around. The restaurant was beautifully decorated and certainly looked successful. There was a family photo of Lom with his wife and two pretty teenage daughters on one wall. On the other walls, there were paintings by Chinese-American painters. Jay knew about Chinese-American art; his mother had been an art teacher and she had given Jay a love of good paintings. He had a pretty good collection of small paintings in his apartment. Now Jay noticed a painting by the famous Milton Quon on the wall behind Lom.

"Looking at the Quon?" said Lom.

"Yes," said Jay. "I love Quon."

"This is a copy, as you can see."

"Yes, I see that." said Jay. "And you have the original . . ."

"In my home," finished Lom. He looked satisfied with himself.

"Very nice," Jay agreed. He hoped that one day he would own one of Quon's pictures himself.

"Well," said Lom, "it's worth a lot of money." He was smiling.

Jay guessed that Lom didn't really understand the painting; he didn't even like it. For Lom, it was just another way of making money, another way to show how successful he was, just dollars. Everyone in San Francisco knew that Lom would do anything for money.

"Do I look like a man who needs to worry about a recipe for fish, hey, Jay boy?" he said and hit Jay on his back, like they were old friends.

Jay didn't say anything, and Lom went on. "The thing is . . ." he said. He leaned toward Jay as if he were telling him a secret, and Jay could feel his breath. "You know how it is here. A lot of competition among the restaurants. Maybe Louie had another fight with someone."

It was true, thought Jay. There were a lot of restaurants in San Francisco, and they all wanted to be the best.

"And you know," said Lom lightly, "fathers don't always tell their children everything." Jay looked at him. Lom continued, "I mean, you know, it could be just something he doesn't want to talk to you about." Then Lom looked up at his family photograph on the wall. "I don't tell my daughters everything I do. Of course not! Or my wife, hey Jay?" Lom laughed and hit Jay on the back again. Then he stood up as if the meeting were over.

Jay got up, too. As he reached out his hand to Lom, he saw the local newspaper, the *San Francisco Chronicle*, on the desk. It was open at a page, Jay noticed, which said, "Wu back in

San Francisco." Wu, thought Jay. The name sounded familiar. There was a photograph next to the article, but Jay could only see the top of a man's head. He'd buy the newspaper on the street, he thought. He didn't really want to spend any more time with Lom.

Jay shook Bernard Lom's hand and stepped out of the Jade Harbor and into the street. What an unpleasant little man, he thought. He was happy to be away from him. Jay's car was parked a little way down the street and he walked toward it. He could hear the sea birds crying and smell the fresh ocean air; it felt good to clear his head after talking to Lom. Yes, the man was unpleasant. Jay wondered if the restaurant owner maybe knew something that he wasn't saying. What was all that about fathers not telling their children everything? Maybe it was nothing, just Lom's little joke. Still, Jay didn't trust him at all.

Jay got in his car and drove along the Embarcadero to Rincon Park. He needed a short walk through the park, he thought; it was a good place to think. Then he'd buy that newspaper. But as he got out of the car, he heard a voice from across the street.

"Jay!"

It was a voice that Jay knew. He looked over to see Tony Lee, Louie's main chef at The Golden Duck. Tony was dressed in his chef's clothes; under his thick blue coat Jay could see the blue and white pants.

"Tony! How are you?" said Jay, as he walked across the street. Tony was an old friend. They were close friends as teenagers, but they didn't see each other very often these days. They lived in different worlds now.

"Oh, I'm good," said Tony, smiling. "You haven't been around the restaurant for a long time." Tony's brown eyes looked into Jay's.

"Well, you know my father," said Jay. "He wants to retire and he wants me to manage the restaurant. It's always a fight." Jay gave a thin smile.

"Yeah, I know how it is," said Tony. "But you're doing very well as an investigator. It's great that you're going your own way. Nice suit by the way!"

Jay was wearing a smart black suit and light blue shirt. "Thanks," he said. "Where are you going?"

"I'm just going to buy some food for the restaurant at the big store near here," Tony replied. "Louie's getting a little old to do that."

"Thanks, Tony," Jay said to his childhood friend. "It's good to know you're there. My father really needs you."

"Yeah, well, you know how it is. I owe Louie a lot," Tony said.

Jay knew how it was. Tony's parents, Kim and Jessica, died in a car accident in 1992, when Tony was just sixteen years old. His uncles and aunts lived in New York, and Tony didn't want to leave his school and his friends in San Francisco. Jay's mother and father were Tony's neighbors on Commercial Street. They felt sorry for the boy. Jay's mother took him into their home. Tony lived with Jay

and his parents until he was eighteen. It seemed that it was the best for him. When Tony left school, Louie gave him a job in the restaurant and taught him how to cook. Now he was a very good chef, one of the best in Chinatown.

Jay looked at Tony. He looked the same as ever. Around his neck, as usual, he wore a gold chain with a gold circle on it—a pendant. The gold circle had the names of his parents on it: Kim and Jessica Lee.

"I'm happy that we've met, Tony," said Jay. "To tell you the truth, I'm a little worried."

"About what?" asked Tony.

"About the fire at The Golden Duck," Jay replied. "About my father really . . ."

Tony looked serious. "Yeah, I saw the fire damage, too," he said.

"Who could have done it, Tony?" Jay asked. "Do you know anybody who doesn't like my father?"

Tony shook his head. "No," he said, "I really can't think of anyone."

"No one at all?" asked Jay.

"No. Your father's an important man in Chinatown, and I think everyone respects him," said Tony.

Jay hoped that it was true, but he knew that in Chinatown anybody as successful as his father probably had more than one enemy.

"He's done so well, and everyone seems to look up to him," Tony went on.

Jay looked at Tony. "Tony, I wish . . ."

"What?" asked Tony.

"I wish Louie would retire now and let you manage the restaurant for him. He's getting old," Jay said.

"Yeah," Tony replied. "Me too, but you know how Louie is. He says it's a Kwan business and . . ."

Jay knew how it was. In Chinatown, businesses were always passed on within the family.

"Don't worry, Jay," said Tony, as he started to walk away. "I'm here, and nothing will happen."

They said good-bye, and Jay walked quickly into the park. Well, at least Tony was looking after his father, he thought.

He started to think about what was happening. What information did he have so far? Not a lot. Just a feeling that he didn't quite trust Bernard Lom and that his father wasn't telling him everything. The air from the ocean was cold, thought Jay, as he pulled his coat around him to keep warm. Then the note left in his father's kitchen came into his head: "I know," it had said. What exactly did the writer of the note know about his father?

Chapter 5

Louie gets mad

Jay walked back toward his car, took out his cell phone, and called his father.

"How is everything?" Jay asked.

There was silence.

"Father, there'll be a security guard starting tonight," Jay said.

"I told you that I didn't want you to do anything!" Louie shouted.

"It's OK," said Jay. "Calm down; no one will see him. You'll have security around the restaurant. And at home, you still have your old gun there, don't you?

"Yes, yes," said Louie, impatiently.

Louie had had the same gun for twenty years. He kept it in a drawer in his living room.

"What about the kitchen?" Jay continued. "Has it been repaired?"

"It's good," said Louie. "Good as new. It was repaired this morning." Louie didn't offer his son any more information.

Jay changed the subject. "I saw Tony," he said carefully.

Louie didn't speak.

It was so hard to get Louie to talk, thought Jay. "He seems very helpful," he said.

"Yes, he is."

"Father, I . . ." Jay tried to look for the right words. In the end he said, "I worry about you."

"Well, you don't need to," said Louie.

"I . . . umm . . . about Tony . . . ," Jay continued. "I know he's not in the family . . ."

"So?" said his father.

"Well, I'm still wondering if you think he could manage The Golden Duck after you retire," Jay finished.

"Are you asking me again to give The Golden Duck to someone who isn't a Kwan?" Louie asked.

"Like I said, I'm worried about you," said Jay. "I don't want your work to be wasted. Tony will take good care of the restaurant. I know he will. Father, if you . . ."

"No! We've talked about this before," Louie said. "Tony is not a Kwan!"

"I just thought that it might be a good idea to . . ."

"You are trying to give your responsibility to Tony!" Louie said.

"But, Father . . ."

"And you're getting involved in things you don't know anything about!" Louie added.

"But I'm really just . . ."

"No!" Louie shouted, "I asked you to manage The Golden Duck! You are my son . . ."

This was hopeless, thought Jay. His father was just getting more and more angry. "OK, calm down, Father," he said. "You don't have to do anything that you don't want to do. I'll talk to you later."

Jay put his phone in his pocket. The old man really was impossible. He thought again about the note. "I know," it had said. What was there to know? Even Bernard Lom had said something about fathers and children. Was his father hiding something? He could be hiding something, even from his son. Jay had never found his father easy; he'd been much closer to his mother, Lucy, who had died ten years before. She'd been the only one who knew how to talk to his father, thought Jay.

Jay sat for a while looking at the ocean. It was true that his father was far from easy, but the more he thought about it, the more Jay felt that he had to discover who was doing this to him. His father was stubborn, but Jay was stubborn, too. They were alike in that way.

Jay remembered the newspaper he had seen in the Jade Harbor. He walked across the street and bought the *San Francisco Chronicle*. Then he walked back to his car and started looking through it for the headline he had seen on Lom's desk. There it was. At the bottom of one of the inside pages there was a small article with the headline "Wu back in San Francisco."

Jay looked closer. Yes, he knew that name. And now he could see the photograph of Harry Wu. The article said that Wu had been allowed to leave jail early. Fifteen years seemed like a short time for murder, but it wasn't unusual in California, Jay thought. Now Wu was on parole. That meant that he had to stay out of trouble, otherwise he'd be back in jail. According to the newspaper, Wu had said that he was going to start a new life.

"Harry Wu," Jay said to himself. He quickly started his car and drove back to Chinatown.

Chapter 6

A quiet life

It had all happened fifteen years ago. Wu had been an important man in Chinatown at that time. He was a violent criminal, but he was successful. He got money from a lot of people, protection money. "Pay me or I'll destroy your business," was his usual way. Fred Chan was a friend of Louie in Chinatown; Chan had a small restaurant, too. Harry Wu tried to get money from Chan, Chan couldn't pay, and Harry Wu killed him. Louie was out late one night and had seen the murder; he was in the wrong place at the wrong time. Louie told the police what he saw and Harry Wu went to jail for fifteen years. End of story. Or maybe not, thought Jay. Could Wu be threatening his father?

Anyway, Jay thought, he should see if Wu was here and what he was doing. If Wu was here in the city, as the newspaper said, Jay guessed he would be in Chinatown.

The traffic was heavy as he drove past the Chinatown Gate. It was always difficult to drive around here, but Jay knew the area well. He knew its little alleys and its little secrets; it was his world, a world he had loved even as a boy. As a man, he'd spent a long time in other cities, but Chinatown had always been there at the back of his mind. Since he'd come back to it just over a year ago, he knew it was a place he would never leave again. It was dirty and it was tough, but it was his city.

Commercial Street, thought Jay. There were a few bars down there where he knew that Harry Wu used to go in the old days. If Wu was in Chinatown, that was the place to find him. Jay went into three bars. It was hard to get any information about Wu, though. No one knew anything—or at least no one who was talking. It was becoming one of those difficult afternoons. Maybe he should just go back to the office.

Then, just as he was leaving the last bar, the barman said, "Try The Red Door—it's just down the street. That's the place Wu used to go to most." Jay knew The Red Door, and it wasn't a very nice place. But, thought Jay, Harry Wu wasn't a very nice man. At least, he wasn't nice fifteen years ago, and he was sure all those years in jail hadn't made him any nicer. The bar was worth trying, he thought.

Jay went into The Red Door and looked around. He'd only been in there once before, but it was pretty much the same as he remembered it. The wooden floor was dirty and the red leather stools at the bar had probably been there for twenty years. The music on the jukebox in the corner was from the eighties. There was a smell of old food and beer, and at the bar there were two men drinking beer. They were wearing dirty overalls; one of them wore a black baseball cap. Jay sat down next to them and ordered a beer, too. He began talking to the barman, just making conversation.

"I haven't seen you in here before," said the young barman, as he gave Jay his bottle of beer.

"No," said Jay, "I usually go downtown these days. But I have been here before. Your name's Jimmy, isn't it?"

"That's right," said the barman. "You have a good memory."

They carried on talking for a while, about the weather, about the football game, about everything. Then Jay said, "I read in the newspaper that Harry Wu was out of jail."

Nobody spoke, but the man with the black cap moved his head over so that he could listen. Maybe he was just the curious type, thought Jay.

"Didn't he use to come in here, back in the old days?" Jay asked. He spoke a little louder so that the man could hear better.

"Yeah," said Jimmy, "but I haven't seen him here since he got out of jail. Maybe he isn't in Chinatown. People say he's going to live a quiet life . . ."

"Really?"

"That's what I heard," said Jimmy. Jay looked at him. The barman's eyes moved around. He knew something, thought Jay. Harry Wu was out of jail, and the chances were that he was back in Chinatown. Chinatown wasn't that big. If he was here, someone would know where he was. It was just a matter of time, but Jay didn't know how much time he had. The words "this is just the beginning" from the note kept coming into his head.

"It's OK, Jimmy, I'll talk to Mr. Kwan."

Jay knew the voice. He turned around and saw Harry Wu walking toward him from the back of the bar. He knew the voice and he knew the face. When Jay had been growing up in Chinatown, everyone knew that face. Wu was fifteen years older now, and his face was a little thinner, but it was still Wu. The two men drinking beer looked round as Wu sat down next to Jay.

"Give Mr. Kwan another beer," said Harry Wu to the barman.

Jay looked at Wu. There was something different about him, he thought. He was older, more tired somehow. Maybe he really was ready to lead a new life.

"So what can I do for you?" asked Harry Wu.

Jay turned fully around so that he could see Wu's eyes. "Somebody's threatening my father," he said quietly, "and it

"Maybe so," said Harry Wu. "Louie Kwan did a bad thing to me. Everybody in Chinatown knows that." He thought for a while.

Then finally, he said, smiling, "But like Jimmy said, I want to live a quiet life."

"A quiet life?"

"I've been in jail for fifteen years," said Harry Wu, "and jail changes a man, you know. It gives him lot of time to think."

Harry Wu took a drink of his whisky and looked back at Jay. "Yeah, I did my time in jail," he said.

"And what now?" asked Jay.

"I have some money and I have a woman who doesn't want me to spend more time in jail," Wu said, looking into Jay's eyes. "I'm just here for a few days to see some old friends, and then I'm leaving Chinatown forever. And that's the truth, Jay Kwan."

Jay looked at Harry Wu. Was it really true? Was he really going to live a quiet life? Violence and crime had been Harry Wu's life. It was difficult to believe that he knew another way to live. But Jay knew that so much time in jail could often change a man. And he did look different.

Harry Wu stood up. "I have to go," he said, "but you're wasting your time on me." Wu said good-bye to the barman and the two men sitting at the bar. Then he walked to the door and opened it. "Maybe there are other people with something against Louie," he called back to Jay. Then he walked out into the street.

Jay finished his beer and stood up, too.

"He told me he didn't want to talk to anyone," said the barman.

"Yeah, I know. It's OK," said Jay. "Anyway, I'll leave you my card." He took his business card from his inside pocket: Jay Kwan, Private Investigator. He moved his head toward the door where Harry Wu had left the bar. "Just in case . . ."

Harry Wu was just out of jail and would be in big trouble if he tried anything against Louie, but Jay knew he wasn't taking any chances. He walked past the two men at the bar. "You too. If you have any information," he said quietly as he put a business card in front of the man with the black cap, "give me a call." Jay stood at the bar. "Oh, and I pay well for good information," he said. He left the bar and walked down the street.

Bernard Lom and Harry Wu, thought Jay. So far there were two men with something against Louie. And it was still only four o'clock.

Chapter 7

At The Golden Duck

"OK," said Amy as Jay walked through the door of the office. "The security guard's fixed for tonight. I told them the situation."

"Good," said Jay. "And the handwriting on the note? What did Sonny Lo say?"

"Well," she answered, "you know Sonny. The usual. The writer is controlling, he said."

"Controlling?" Jay shook his head. "Don't all criminals like to control other people?"

Amy smiled. "Yeah, maybe." She got up to leave. "What about your afternoon?"

"Interesting," he said, "and enough Chinatown bars to last for the next year!" Jay told her about his meetings with Lom and with Harry Wu, and then he said, "I'm going to the The Golden Duck this evening to see how things are with my father. Do you want to come with me?"

"OK," Amy said. "It'll be good see The Golden Duck." She hadn't grown up in San Francisco. She still didn't know some of its famous places.

"Good," Jay said. "The food's great, too. Let's hope my father's friendly!"

At 7:30 Jay met Amy near the Chinatown Gate. It wasn't far from the restaurant so they decided to walk. It was a fine evening, but cold. They talked as they walked. "So how did you become an investigator?" she asked him.

"Well," said Jay, "I studied law at Stanford University, and I spent two years working as a lawyer in Los Angeles. But I didn't want to be a lawyer. I guess I didn't want to be at a desk every day. One day, I met a private investigator and I liked the idea, you know, the search for the truth. It kind of suits me . . . a bit like you."

Jay knew that Amy had been to law school in New York, and then had come out to San Francisco to be with a boyfriend. She'd stayed when the boyfriend had gone. Like Jay, she liked the excitement of being an investigator.

They arrived at The Golden Duck. Jay and Amy went through the big gold door of the restaurant and looked for a waiter to show them to a table. The restaurant was large and very well decorated. It was almost full of people; it was obvious that Louie Kwan's business was very successful.

"Put us near the window, please," said Jay to the waiter, "and tell my father that we're here, please." The waiter led them to a small table near the window and lit the long white candles.

A few moments later Louie appeared. He looked angrily at Jay, but he couldn't really have a fight with him in front of Amy and everyone in the restaurant.

"You must eat the Peking Duck tonight," Louie said to Amy. "It's very, very good. I made it myself. And afterwards come and see us in the kitchen."

Jay ordered the Peking Duck and a lot of different types of food. Soon, he and Amy were eating Louie's delicious food.

"Mmm," said Amy, smiling. "This is the best Peking Duck in the world!"

"So," said Jay, "you didn't grow up here, but you're just like everyone in Chinatown now! Everyone here loves food."

Amy laughed and asked him about The Golden Duck.

He told her the story of the Kwan family and the restaurant.

"And you've become a private investigator," said Amy. "I can see why your father is unhappy."

"I've always wanted to do it for myself," said Jay seriously, "you know, have my own business, my own successful career. I mean, somehow it's too easy just to take over your father's business . . ."

Amy nodded. "I know what you mean," she said.

Jay waited for her to speak.

"My mother was a lawyer," Amy went on. "She wanted to be a judge, but in those days it was hard for women to do that . . . so she thought her only daughter could do it instead."

"But you didn't want to . . . ," Jay said.

"Right," said Amy.

"So you know how I feel," said Jay. "In some ways I feel bad about it. I know how important it is to him . . ."

Amy nodded.

"There's a part of me that wants to just do what he wants," Jay went on, "but in other ways . . . I'm just as proud as he is. And I'm stubborn."

"I noticed," said Amy smiling.

"Well, I guess it's not a bad thing for a private investigator. Want some coffee?"

After dinner, Jay and Amy went into the kitchen of The Golden Duck.

"Thank you," said Amy to Louie. "It was wonderful—the best food I've ever tasted!"

Louie smiled at Amy and he suddenly looked ten years younger. Food was his life, and he was happy when people really liked it. "Good!" he said. "And you should meet everyone who works here. This is Micki Cheung. He's a new chef. He just started two months ago, but he's going to be very good." Micki was about twenty-five years old; he was a tall young man with a big smile.

"And this is Tony Lee," Louie went on. "Tony has been here since he was sixteen."

Tony was busy making sure that the young chefs cleaned the kitchen at the end of the evening, but he stopped to say hello to Amy.

"And Jay," said Louie, pointing his finger at his son, "he doesn't want anything to do with the restaurant." The old man shook his head.

"Let's go," said Jay to Amy, as he moved her toward the door. He didn't want to get into the usual conversation. "Everything's OK, I guess?"

Louie didn't say anything, but nodded his head.

"I heard today that Harry Wu is out of jail," said Jay to his father, as he was leaving. He didn't say anything to Louie about the meeting with Wu at The Red Door.

"Really?" said Louie. His face hardly moved. It was hard for Jay to tell if he knew already, or even cared. Yet Jay knew that Louie had to feel something about Harry Wu. After all, Louie was the one who was responsible for sending him to jail.

It was late and outside it was even colder than before. Jay called a cab and they rode back to Amy's apartment through the dark streets.

At her apartment, Amy started to get out of the cab. Then she suddenly said, "Oh!"

"What is it?" asked Jay.

"It's my purse!" she said. "I think I left it in the restaurant, in the kitchen."

"Well, that's OK," said Jay. "I can get it and bring it tomorrow."

"But it's got my door key in it," said Amy. "I have to get it tonight."

"No problem," said Jay. "Driver, take us back to The Golden Duck." They drove back to the restaurant. Jay took out his cell phone and tried to phone his father, but the phone line was busy. He looked at his watch. It was 11:30. "Oh well, never mind," he thought to himself. "The purse must be there and it will only take a few minutes."

Five minutes later they were outside the restaurant. Jay knew that the front door would be closed by now, but the kitchen door would still be open. The kitchen was round the back of the restaurant. "Wait here in the cab," he said to Amy, "and I'll go round the back."

Jay ran round into the alley, the small street at the back of The Golden Duck. He stood at the top of the alley; it was very dark. There was no one there. He looked at his watch; the security guard would start work in half an hour. Yes, the kitchen light was still on. He walked quickly toward the door. Then suddenly the back door opened and a man walked out. It looked like Tony. Yes, it was Tony, and he looked very angry. Jay didn't go closer, but watched from the darkness.

"Are you crazy?" Louie asked from inside. "Where did you get this?"

Tony said something that Jay couldn't hear. Then he shut the kitchen door quickly, making a loud noise.

"Tony!!" Louie shouted. "It's not like you think!"

"What is it like then?" shouted Tony, but he didn't wait to hear the answer.

Jay watched as Tony turned and ran in the opposite direction. He waited until Tony was gone; then he went in the back door and into the kitchen. Only Louie was there. The waiters and the other kitchen staff had already gone. Louie was getting ready to go home. He lived in the expensive Nob Hill area of the city now and he always drove home around this time. His face was serious, but he didn't say anything.

"What's wrong with Tony?" Jay asked his father.

"Oh nothing . . . it's just very late," said Louie. He turned away.

"But he was very angry," Jay said.

"Leave it!" his father shouted, turning back and looking angrily at his son.

Jay knew that it was no use trying again. He told Louie about Amy's purse, and they both looked for it. It had fallen behind a table. Jay picked it up, said goodnight to his father, and went back to the cab.

Amy looked at his face and could see that there was something wrong. "What is it?" she asked as they drove off.

"Oh, it's probably nothing," he said, "but I just saw my father and Tony shouting at each other." Jay described what he had seen in the alley. He didn't tell her exactly what he'd heard, though. He was still trying to understand it himself.

"Do they usually argue?" asked Amy.

"No . . . I mean, when I saw Tony the other day he seemed really friendly with Louie," said Jay, "really helpful." He added, "But I guess I don't really know. I don't often see them together these days." Jay told her about how his parents had taken Tony into their home when he was sixteen.

"Your mother and father adopted him? He became a son?"

"No, not legally," Jay explained, "but he lived with us for two years. He went to school in San Francisco and it seemed like the best idea. My father trained him to be a chef. My mother really treated him like a son, I think . . ."

"So why doesn't Tony take over The Golden Duck?" asked Amy. "I mean, be the owner? You said that your father wants to retire soon and he's trained Tony. So . . .?"

"When I ask my father about it he gets angry and says that Tony is not his son and it's a real family business, a Kwan business," said Jay. "That's the way in Chinatown. He says Tony's the wrong type, too, but I think it's just an excuse."

"An excuse?"

"You know, to make me feel bad," said Jay. "He says it's my responsibility, not Tony's." Jay's face became thoughtful.

Jay and Amy said goodnight. Jay went home and went to bed, but he couldn't sleep. "Where did you get this?" his father had asked Tony. What was "this"? What had Tony and his father been arguing about? Jay couldn't sleep. All night he thought about what he'd heard that evening.

Chapter 8

A talk

The next morning Jay was still thinking about the night before. What was the fight between Tony and Louie about? "It's not like you think!" Louie had said. What did Tony think? There was no way that Jay could ask Louie directly. He knew that Louie would just say it was nothing, as usual. Jay would talk to Tony later.

"OK," he said to Amy, trying to forget about the fight between Louie and Tony. "Let's start with who could be threatening my father." Jay stood up and started walking up and down the office.

"So far we have Lom and Wu," he said. "Why Lom?" He answered his own question. "There's a history of bad feeling between them. Lom has a reason to hate Louie that was never really resolved. He's also unpleasant, and I don't really trust him." He paused, then asked, "Why not Lom? Because he seems to have left his fight with Louie behind." He looked at Amy: "Why Wu?"

"Because he has a real reason to hate Louie," Amy replied. "Fifteen years in jail!"

"Why not Wu?" Jay asked, then answered his own question. "Because he's just out of jail, so he would be stupid to get into trouble."

"Criminals aren't usually stupid," said Amy.

"Mmm . . ." Jay said thoughtfully. "One thing is certain—if he wanted to pay my father back, he probably wouldn't do it himself."

He gave Amy a list of places in Chinatown and asked her to see if Harry Wu was there.

"Follow him a little, see what he's really doing, who he's talking to."

"OK," said Amy.

"He says he's ready for the quiet life," said Jay, "but we'll see if it's true. Let's see exactly what he's doing around Chinatown."

Amy would go to Chinatown, sit in her car in the street, and just watch. Watch and wait. If she saw Wu, she would follow him. It was hard, boring work, and the chance of seeing Wu was very low. But this was what detective work was like usually, and it often got results.

Jay was in his office when the phone rang later that afternoon.

"Yes," answered Jay.

"Umm, Mr. Kwan? My name's Jackson," said the man. "We met yesterday in the bar, The Red Door. I was with my friend, having a drink. I was wearing a black baseball cap . . . do you remember me?"

Twenty-four hours. Not bad, thought Jay.

"Oh yes," he said. "What is it?"

"Harry Wu. You were talking to him."

"Yes, go on." said Jay.

Half an hour later, Jay was in Union Square. It was one of the busiest places in the city, and in the late afternoon there were lots of people walking through it on their way home from work. Jay sat on a bench in the middle of the square and waited for Jackson.

"Mr. Kwan!"

Jay turned around. It was Jackson; he was wearing the same dirty overalls and baseball cap he had been wearing in the bar, and he was out of breath.

"So what do you have?" asked Jay.

"It'll cost you two hundred dollars," the man replied.

"Two hundred dollars?"

"The thing is, I've got a girlfriend," said the man. "Very expensive."

"I'll give you a hundred and fifty," said Jay, "but it had better be good. I'll give you fifty now, and the rest if you give me anything useful."

Jay took fifty dollars out of his wallet.

"Well," said the man, taking the money quickly and putting it in his pocket. "I saw him this morning."

"Yes?"

"In a café over on the other side of the city."

"Which café?"

"The Black Cat."

Jay knew the café he was talking about. "And?" he asked.

"Well, he was there . . ."

"Listen, Mr. Jackson," Jay said quietly in the man's ear, "if you are wasting my time I'm not going to be very happy, and that means no money."

"OK, OK," said the man. "He was talking to someone."

"Someone?"

"Yes," said the man. "I think it was that guy, the chef at The Golden Duck."

"Who do you mean? The old man? Louie?" asked Jay.

"No, not the old man, one of the younger guys. I don't know his name, but he works at The Golden Duck. In the kitchen."

"What did he look like, this younger guy?" Jay asked.

"I can't say really, just a young Chinese guy. Tall. Short black hair. I just know he's one of the chefs there. And they were having a serious talk."

Jay looked at him and waited.

"The young guy jumped up and ran off," said the man, "and he looked really mad. Really angry, you know. "

"Can you remember anything about the young man. Anything at all?" he asked.

"No . . . ," said Jackson, "but I do know that Wu gave him a piece of paper. A letter, maybe. Something like that."

"Anything else?"

Jackson thought for a while. "No . . . not really," he said finally. "Listen, I'm sorry but I have to go." He looked toward the place where Jay's wallet was. "I have a problem at home."

"OK," said Jay, shaking his head. He took his wallet from his inside pocket and gave the man a hundred dollars. "But if you remember anything else, you know where to find me."

"OK," said Jackson. "Any more money?"

"Listen," said Jay. "If you know anything else, you'd better tell me now, because you're already making me mad, Mr. Jackson."

"OK, OK," said Jackson. "I can't remember anything right now." He got up and walked away.

Jay walked quickly toward his car. Jackson! Jay couldn't believe that the man was trying to get even more money out of him. Still, Jay had something. He got in his car and drove away from Union Square. There were only two chefs apart from Louie at The Golden Duck, he thought. Both of them were young. One of them was Micki Cheung; the other was Tony Lee. Both of them had short black hair; both were tall. One of them was talking to Harry Wu about something important. Something that made Cheung or Lee really mad.

Which one of them was talking to Wu? And what was that conversation about?

Chapter 9

Danger

Jay didn't know much about Micki Cheung. He had started at The Golden Duck about two months before. He was a pleasant young man, and Louie seemed happy with him and his work. When Jay saw Cheung and his father together, Cheung always seemed respectful to the older man. As far as Jay knew, Cheung didn't know Wu at all.

Back at the office he made a few calls to people he knew in Chinatown, asking them about Cheung. Nobody had anything bad to say about him; he seemed clean. Jay knew there was no point in talking to Tony. What next?

Around six o'clock, the phone rang. It was Jackson. "I remembered a small thing, Mr. Kwan," he said.

"I'm listening," said Jay.

"Well," he said, "the young Chinese man had a gold pendant around his neck—a kind of gold circle. I don't know whether it's important . . ."

"A circle?" asked Jay.

"Yes, that's right."

"Thank you very much, Mr. Jackson." Jay said. "I owe you."

Maybe Jackson wasn't that bad after all, Jay thought. A gold pendant. Tony. It had to be Tony! He tried to remember if Cheung wore a pendant, but he couldn't. Jay called Amy and told her what Jackson had told him. "I'm pretty sure Micki Cheung wasn't wearing a pendant when we were at

The Golden Duck," Amy said. "And I do remember Tony's. I noticed it because it's quite unusual."

"It had to be Tony Lee," Jay said. He put the phone down. Tony and Harry Wu, he thought. What was that about?

"I'm going to talk to Tony right now," he thought. Maybe it was nothing. Maybe it was just something between Tony and Wu. Anyway, he had to find out. He found Tony's number and rang it. Tony's voice said, "Leave a message." Jay didn't leave a message. He rang Louie.

Jay was happy to hear that his father was OK. It was Tony's evening off and Louie thought that he was at home. "I'm going home soon, too," said Louie. "Micki's here and I'm feeling tired tonight." Monday was always a quiet night at The Golden Duck.

Jay rang Tony's number again. Still no Tony. Maybe I should go and talk to him, Jay thought. He thought about Tony Lee. First there was the fight between Tony and his father, when Jay had heard Tony say such strange things. Why had Tony been so mad at his father? What, or who, were they arguing about? Then Tony and Wu. They'd talked. Again Tony was mad. Jay tried to remember if he'd ever seen Tony so mad, but he couldn't. But now he'd been really mad twice in two days!

When Jay saw Tony just the other day, it seemed as if Tony really cared for Louie. "Don't worry, Jay," Tony had said, "I'm here, and nothing will happen." But that was before he talked to Wu! Maybe there was a simple explanation for it all? Maybe he just needed to talk to Tony. Jay ran downstairs and got into his car.

Jay called Tony's number again. Still he heard Tony's voice but there was no Tony. Where was he? Tony was mad because of something Wu had said to him, Jay thought.

And Wu had given him something—a letter maybe. Maybe he was still mad. Wu and Tony. Someone like Wu would be clever enough to get someone else to do his dirty work, Jay thought. Then he thought of Sonny Lo's words when he looked at the note that had been left in Louie's kitchen. Controlling, he had said. Controlling.

Ten minutes later, Jay arrived outside Tony's apartment at Waverly Place. He hadn't been here for many years, but it all looked so familiar. He looked up at the second floor where Tony's apartment was; the lights were on. He tried phoning Tony again, but it was still a recorded message. Jay got out of his car and ran up the stairs to Tony's door. A light had broken, and the hallway outside Tony's apartment was dark. As he walked toward the door, it opened suddenly, and he saw Tony's face come out from the darkness. Tony was leaving, and he was in a hurry.

"Tony!" Jay said.

Tony was surprised and ran straight into him.

Jay could see that he was mad. "Tony . . . I . . ."

Tony pulled Jay to him and said in his ear, "Get out of my way!!" Tony's voice was quiet, almost a whisper, but it sounded vicious, cruel. It didn't sound like Tony at all.

"I need to talk to you, Tony," Jay said.

Tony threw Jay against the wall violently and hit him hard around his head. Jay saw everything go dark as he fell to the ground.

Jay tried to move his arms, his legs. His head hurt very badly. The floor beneath him was very hard. He tried to think. Then he remembered Tony. Tony had hit him. He was on the floor outside Tony's apartment. How long had he been there on the floor? He looked at his watch but it

was too dark. Slowly he got to his feet and went downstairs. When he got near the outside door, in the hallway he saw a piece of paper, just lying on the floor. What was it, Jay wondered. Tony may have dropped it in his hurry to leave. Jay picked it up. He needed to find some light so that he could see the paper. He got into his car and turned on the light, his head still painful. He looked at his watch. Nine thirty. Good . . . he'd only been on the floor for fifteen minutes.

He looked quickly at the piece of paper that he'd picked up. The note said, "Here's the evidence you were looking for." He recognized the writing in the note—it looked like the same handwriting as the note that had been left in his father's kitchen after the fire!

Evidence? What evidence? thought Jay. Was it the letter that Wu had given him? No, there must be something else. Tony must have something with him. Something that someone had left for Tony, with the note. Evidence. Evidence of what?

Jay put the note on the seat next to him. He looked at his watch; it was 9:35. He hoped he wasn't too late. Jay drove as quickly as he could to Louie's house on Nob Hill.

Chapter 10

A bad night

Jay had a short metal bar in his car, the kind used by thieves to open windows. He wished he still had a key to Louie's house, but he didn't. He took the bar, put the note inside his jacket and got out of his car. He could hear voices as he ran up to Louie's big house. The neighborhood was a wealthy one, and Louie's house stood alone, with a large garden around it. Jay ran round the back quietly. Louie's bedroom was on the ground floor. Jay tried the two windows. One was locked. He tried the second one. It was also locked. He took the metal bar and carefully put it into the edge of the window. Quietly and carefully he pushed, trying to open the window. Seconds passed, but the lock didn't break.

Jay breathed heavily. He could hear voices inside the house, getting louder. He pushed again. Finally, after what seemed like hours, the lock broke. He pushed the window open and climbed through it as quietly as he could. He walked past Louie's bed in the darkness and went toward his father's living room.

"You killed them," he heard Tony's voice from the living room as he approached.

"No!" Louie sounded scared, Jay thought. Jay knew that Tony would know where Louie's gun was. After all, Louie had kept it in the same place for years. Jay had to do something. And now.

"Tony." Jay opened the door and went into the room calmly.

He saw Tony with Louie's gun in his hand. Tony was red, breathing heavily. Louie was standing on the other side of the room. He looked terrified.

Tony, surprised, moved back so that he could cover Jay with the gun, too. "Jay . . . what a surprise. Come in," said Tony. "You should hear this!"

"Tony . . ."

"Shut up and listen, Jay," Tony said. Then he said to Louie, "You loved my mother. This is your handwriting, isn't it?" He was holding a letter in his hand.

Louie didn't move or speak.

"It's true isn't it?" Tony said, pointing the gun at Louie. "It's true that you loved her?" Tony was shouting now. "Come on, tell me! Tell me the truth."

Finally, Louie nodded his head. Jay watched, hardly believing what he was hearing.

Jay waited for Louie's reply. "Yes," the old man said finally.

"My father found out, didn't he?" Tony went on.

Louie didn't say anything.

"There was a fight, and you decided to kill him," Tony added. "And you killed my mother by mistake—she was in the car!"

"I told you that it wasn't like that!" Louie said.

"Yes, it was," Tony shouted back. "You've always pretended that you loved me, but really you just felt guilty that you killed my parents!"

"Tony!"

"Shut up, Jay!"

"This explains everything," Tony went on. "You didn't really love me at all, so why give me the restaurant?"

"But . . . of course I did," said Louie. "But why would I kill your parents?" asked Louie, also trying to calm Tony. "You must know I didn't."

"Because I have the evidence!"

"What evidence?" Louie asked. "The letter doesn't prove anything . . . "

"You had a fight with my father," said Tony. "People saw it. The day after the fight, he died in the car accident. There was a police report. It said that someone had played with the brakes. I have the police report here! They never found the man who did it, but I know it was you!"

"But that's not true!!" Louie said.

"You know you did it!" Tony went on. "You wanted to kill my father because he found out that you loved my mother! It all makes sense!"

"Tony . . ." Jay tried again to calm Tony, who was now so angry that he was shaking. "Is this Harry Wu . . . Is he the one that told you all this?"

"It doesn't matter who told me!" said Tony. "It's true . . . and he knows it!!" Tony pointed the gun at Louie.

"But Harry Wu," said Jay, "he's telling lies! After all, my father put him in jail."

"Go away!" said Tony. "Look at the evidence!"

"But think, Tony," said Jay. "How would Wu get a police report? Let's just talk about this!"

"Let's just talk about this?" said Tony, turning toward Jay. "Yes, I guess you would like to know why he did that to your mother!" Tony threw the two pieces of paper at Jay. They fell to the floor in front of him.

Jay moved to pick the papers up. As he bent down, Tony shouted, "You killed them. Now I'll kill you!"

"Tony!" Jay shouted, and then, "Father!"

Jay looked on, shocked, as Tony pointed the gun at Louie. Jay looked at Louie and heard a shot and suddenly Louie was lying on the floor. Jay moved toward his father. Tony stood there, as if surprised by what he had done. Then he turned the gun toward Jay. Jay froze. But at the last minute it seemed that Tony couldn't do it. He brought his arm down and ran out of the door.

Jay ran over to his father and sat down on the floor beside him. "Father . . ."

"I . . . my son," Louie said softly looking at the door. Then there was silence as Louie's eyes closed.

Chapter 11

I loved her

Later, at the hospital, the doctor showed Jay to Louie's room. Louie was still in a coma.

Jay looked at his father, then turned to the doctor. "Will he . . . ?"

"We don't know if he'll live," said the young doctor. "He's not young, and the wound is near his heart. We just have to wait at this stage."

The sickness in Jay's stomach rose. He took a deep breath. He and the doctor walked out of Louie's room.

"Listen," he said to the doctor. "Please don't tell the police yet."

"But I have to, sir," said the doctor. "Your father was attacked."

"Look," he said. "I'm an investigator. Someone is trying to kill my father. When they find out he's still alive . . . "

"I understand, but you'll have to talk to the police," said the doctor. "It's not my decision."

Jay thought that he had to act quickly. If Wu found out that Louie was still alive, he'd kill him. He had to talk to Louie and get to Tony before the police did. But Louie was asleep, in a coma. It was impossible to talk to him.

He remembered the pieces of paper that Tony had thrown at him. Jay had them in his pocket, and now he took them out. One was the letter. He recognized Louie's writing. Jay looked at it. It was from Louie to Jessica Lee. The date was

October 1975. Though Tony had said that it was a love letter, still Jay could hardly believe his eyes when he read it.

"Darling Jessica," the letter said. He read down the page. "I love you very much. One day we will be together, and it may be sooner than you think." Jay's eyes went down to the bottom of the page. "Your Louie," it said. And it was his father's writing!

Jay's mind was filled with thoughts. Did Louie love Jessica? But what about Jay's mother? Louie . . . Jay felt terrible. How could his father do such a thing? But it was his father's writing . . . Jay thought about his father and his face became very serious. What if it was all true? What if his father really was a killer?

Jay looked at the other piece of paper. It was a police report. It was from Kim and Jessica Lee's accident, the one that killed them in November 1992. Jay read down the paper. Cause of accident: brake failure. Then the police officer's note next to it: "Cut brake lines. Not an accident. Investigate." Investigate, thought Jay . . . but there had been no investigation . . .

A nurse called the doctor back into Louie's room. "Doctor, he's awake!"

Jay ran into his father's room with the doctor. They were both surprised; the old man looked almost well.

"It's incredible that he's alive," said the doctor. "Your father is very strong, Mr. Kwan."

"Father," Jay said. "It's OK. I'm here."

"Jay?"

"Yes, it's me, Father." He held his father's arm. "Are you OK?"

The old man was sitting up in bed. "I told you not to get

involved in this," he said. But Jay noticed that Louie wasn't angry.

"It's too late for all that," Jay said seriously. "I have to talk to you."

"Wait a moment, Mr. Kwan," said the young doctor. "Your father needs to rest."

"It's OK, doctor," Jay said. "I just need a few minutes with him."

The doctor looked at Louie Kwan. "Well, OK," he said. "But just a few minutes." He left the room.

"Father," Jay said gently. He didn't know how to tell his father how happy he was that he was alive. He gave him a drink of water. Finally, he said, "I need to talk to you about all this."

"Yes?" asked Louie.

Jay held the two pieces of paper in front of Louie.

"Tell me about this," he said, seriously.

"I . . ."

"You . . . and Jessica Lee," said Jay.

"Yes," said Louie. "It's true . . . I . . ."

Jay's heart felt heavy. Even after seeing the letter, he had hoped that none of it was true.

"I . . . loved your mother, Jay . . . I . . ."

"You loved my mother," said Jay, "but you also loved Jessica Lee. That's what it says in this letter."

"Yes, I did," said Louie sadly. "I'm sorry, Jay . . ."

"But how . . .?"

"These things happen in a man's life," said Louie.

Jay looked at his father.

"But I want you to listen carefully, Jay," Louie continued. "I didn't kill Kim Lee. Of course I didn't. I'm not a killer, Jay. You know me!"

"But the police report . . ."

"You must believe me," said Louie, sitting up straight. He looked his son in the eye. He took Jay's hand and held it tight. "You must believe me," he repeated.

"I do, Father," Jay said, "I do." Jay knew his father. He knew that he was stubborn and proud, but he knew that he wasn't a killer. Could the police report not be real?

Louie closed his eyes and lay back on his bed.

Jay went out of Louie's room and again looked at the note that he'd found outside Tony's apartment. "Here's the evidence you were looking for." It was written by the same person who had left the note in Louie's kitchen. Controlling, thought Jay. Controlling. Controlling Tony. Somebody who had a reason to hate Louie. Somebody who wasn't stupid enough to do it himself. Somebody who would use half of the truth to get Tony to kill Louie for him. Someone like Wu would be clever enough to get someone else to do his dirty work, Jay thought.

"Mr. Kwan?" The police officer had arrived and he now walked up to Jay. "Officer King. I have to talk to you about what happened to your father."

"Officer," said Jay, "no one must know that my father is still alive. I need a little time."

The officer looked at Jay. "I can't do that, sir," he said, "and I'll need to talk to you about last night."

Jay showed him his card. "Listen," he said loudly, "I'm an investigator, and believe me, someone is trying to kill my father."

"I understand, sir," said the officer. "Please try to keep calm."

"I just need some time," Jay said, quietly but firmly.

Finally, the officer said, "I'll talk with the captain." And he went to talk to his boss on his radio.

A few moments later Officer King came back and said that no news would go out about Jay's father for the next few hours. "But," he said, "I need to know what happened last night before you go. And from now on you have to work with us. Tell us what's going on. OK?"

"OK," said Jay. He explained everything to Officer King and gave him the police report. Then he ran down the stairs and drove quickly to Tony's apartment at Waverly Place. Tony wasn't a criminal, he thought. He wouldn't know what to do. He would think that Louie was dead, that he'd killed him. Maybe he had run away already. But maybe he was still there, at his apartment, scared, not knowing what to do. Maybe he had told Wu what had happened, and Wu had told Tony that he would help him.

He arrived at Tony's apartment and looked up at the window. He could see nothing at first. Then he picked up a large stone from the side of the road and threw it hard against a garbage can. It made a big noise, and a shadow came to Tony's window. Tony was there, thought Jay.

Jay rang Amy and told her about Louie. "I want you to collect a police report I left at the hospital with Officer King. Take it to Officer Steve Gomez at the San Francisco Police Department. He owes me a favor. Ask him to check it for me. I need to know whether it's a real report or not. But no questions asked."

"OK, I'm on my way," she said.

"Wait. Give me half an hour," Jay went on, "and then get the police to come to Tony Lee's apartment." He gave her

Tony's address. "Get them to bring a few men." Jay could work with the police, but first there was something that he had to do, and it was far too important to leave to the San Francisco Police Department. He had to bring in Harry Wu. And to do that, he needed Tony.

Chapter 12

Bad blood

"Tony!" said Jay. He pushed through the door of Tony's small apartment quickly.

"Go away!!"

"Tony . . . you tried to kill Louie!" said Jay.

"Tried . . .?"

"Louie's alive," said Jay. "You haven't killed him."

"He should die!" shouted Tony. "I was just doing what's right!"

"Harry Wu," Jay said. "He used you." Jay wondered where Tony had put Louie's gun. Had he dropped it somewhere, or was it with him now, here? He moved close to Tony.

Tony moved back. "What are you talking about?"

"He controlled you," said Jay. "He got you to do his dirty work."

"What do you mean?" said Tony. "Yes, Harry Wu gave me the evidence. But it's all true. Louie killed my father and my mother. Then he took me into his house as if I were . . ." Tony's face went red with anger.

Jay went toward Tony. "Think about it," he said. "Louie put Wu in jail for fifteen years. There's a lot of bad blood between them. Of course he wanted to get him! And he found the cruelest way. He found you!"

"Shut up, Jay!" Tony pushed Jay away angrily.

Jay tried to hold Tony, but Tony fought back.

"Tony," said Jay, "I need you to help me get Wu!"

"Go away!" said Tony, hitting Jay around his head.

They fought for some minutes. Jay tried to hold Tony. "Tony, stop!!" he said. "You have to listen to me!"

Tony's face was ugly with anger now. Jay had never seen him like this. "It all makes sense now. That's why Louie didn't want me to have the restaurant. He hated me as much as he hated my father! That's why he always wanted you to have it—even though you don't want it!"

"I'm his son," said Jay. "It's normal. The important thing is that we get Wu."

Tony wasn't listening to Jay. "He hated me!" he went on. "I worked in that restaurant since I was sixteen years old. I worked with Louie every day. I helped him to build his business. Day after day, week after week, year after year."

Jay knew that he had to keep bringing Tony back to Harry Wu.

"Think, Tony," Jay said carefully. "You're going to believe a convicted killer over the man who's been your father for so many years? Because of Harry Wu, you tried to kill my father . . . and now you're going to kill me? Tony, it's me, Jay!"

"We need to get Wu," Jay went on. "You need to help me."

"You just don't understand, do you?" said Tony. "Louie killed my parents!" He pointed the gun at Jay. Jay tried to think.

"The police report," said Jay. "I'm sure it's not real! I'm sure that Harry Wu got one of his men to make a fake police report. I'll prove it to you."

But Tony still wasn't listening. "He killed them!" he shouted. In his anger, Tony tore at the gold chain and pendant around his neck and threw them across the floor.

Suddenly, there was a noise as the door opened. Tony moved quickly as he heard the noise and opened his mouth to speak. His gun was still pointed at Jay.

The door opened and Officer Gomez came in. There was a loud noise as a gun went off. Jay closed his eyes. He felt nothing. When he opened his eyes he saw Tony Lee lying on the floor of the living room.

Jay moved over to Tony and felt his neck gently.

"He's dead."

Chapter 13

Harry Wu

Jay walked slowly across the room and picked up Tony's gold chain and pendant.

The two other police officers came into the room to join Gomez.

"His gun was on you . . . I tried to stop him," said Gomez to Jay.

But Tony had moved suddenly and his own gun had fired by mistake. Tony had shot himself. It was a mistake, a terrible mistake, thought Jay.

Jay slowly put Tony's chain and pendant in his pocket. "Tony, Tony," he said gently.

Jay told Gomez about Harry Wu and Tony Lee. He told him what had happened fifteen years ago.

Jay's face was serious. "Let's get Wu," he said. "This bad blood has gone far enough."

"But how can we prove Wu's part in this," Gomez asked, "now that Tony Lee is dead?"

"What about the police report?" asked Jay.

"It wasn't written by the San Francisco Police Department," said Gomez. "It's a fake. We think it was done by Brad Martin, who was in jail with Wu. Martin had a record for forgery."

"Yes, I thought so," said Jay. "And there's a man called Jackson who saw Tony and Wu together. That was the day when Wu gave Tony the letter, I think." He reached into his pocket. "And there's this note that Wu left for Tony. The handwriting's the same as on the note left in my father's kitchen. I'm pretty sure that it's Wu's."

"But how could he make the mistake of writing the notes himself?" asked Gomez.

"He was in a hurry to kill Louie," said Jay, "and he thought his plan was so clever that everyone would just think it was Tony."

That was the way with criminals, Jay thought. "Criminals aren't usually stupid," Amy had said, but that wasn't quite true. Oh yes, they thought they were very clever, but they weren't. He looked around for Tony's cell phone. He picked it up from the table and looked through the numbers. There were a lot of names there. He looked down the list and found the name he was looking for—Harry Wu. He wrote a message and sent it. "Louie Kwan is dead," it said. "I want to talk. Tony."

A few minutes later there was a "beep beep" sound from Tony Lee's cell phone. It was a message from Harry Wu; he wanted to meet in the park near Washington Street.

Jay and the police officers went to the Washington Street Park. The three officers and Jay stood behind trees and waited. Officer Steve Gomez put a small electronic device on the inside of Jay's jacket to record Wu when he talked. They wanted his voice saying that he was the one who made Tony try to kill Louie.

Twenty minutes later, Wu arrived. Jay walked out into the open, but Officer Gomez and his two men waited.

"Kwan!"

"Surprised to see me?" asked Jay, walking closer to Wu.

Wu didn't reply, but looked around nervously.

"You wanted to kill my father, Wu," Jay went on.

"I . . . I don't know what you're talking about," said Harry Wu.

"I'm talking about murder," said Jay. "You're going back to jail, Wu."

"I don't know what you're talking about," said Wu again.

"You told Tony that Louie Kwan was responsible for the death of his father and mother, didn't you, Wu?" Jay asked.

"I said I have no idea what you're talking about," Wu repeated.

"I think you do," said Jay. "You gave Tony the 'evidence' that you got from an old jail friend—Brad Martin, the forger. But unfortunately the evidence isn't really evidence at all . . . and there are these notes." Jay held the notes that Wu had left for Louie and Tony in his hand.

"They were written by you, weren't they, Wu?" asked Jay.

Wu didn't say anything.

"The letter from my father to Jessica Lee . . ."

"It's a real letter," said Wu. "Your father loved Jessica Lee!"

"Yes, he did," said Jay, "and it is a real letter . . . but the police report's a fake, and I can prove it. Your fingerprints are all over it." Jay knew that with the notes written by Wu and the fake police report he had enough to send Wu back to jail.

"My father is not a killer," Jay went on. "But you are, Wu."

Wu became angry. "It wasn't me," said Wu. "It was Tony who shot him."

"Tony? How did you know that?" asked Jay. " I'll tell you how, Wu. You knew because you gave Tony enough information to make him go to kill him!"

Wu didn't speak, but he'd already said enough.

"Your father . . .?"

"My father is still alive, but poor Tony is not," said Jay. He moved close to Wu. "You caused all this, Wu," he said. "You caused it by telling Tony that Louie killed Kim and Jessica Lee."

"That's just part of it," said Wu. "You don't know anything, Kwan . . ."

Jay looked at Wu's face. "What don't I know?" he asked. He suddenly remembered the note left after the fire in Louie's kitchen. "I know," it had said. "What exactly don't I know?" he repeated.

Wu smiled an unpleasant smile. "Ask your father, Kwan!" he said.

Officer Steve Gomez had heard enough. He walked out from behind the trees with his two officers. "Come on, Wu," he said. "We're going to the police station to talk about the fire at The Golden Duck and everything else."

Jay opened his jacket and showed Wu the recording device he had used to record him. Wu looked shocked.

"You know something, Wu?" Jay asked.

"What?"

"It looks like you're going to have that quiet life after all," he said. "In jail."

"Yes," added Gomez. "You're going back to jail . . . and this time it will be for a very long time."

Jay stood and watched through the window as the police officers put Harry Wu in the police car. Wu had broken his parole, and he was definitely going back to jail. But Tony was dead. He touched Tony Lee's chain and pendant in his pocket and felt a great sadness in his heart. The bad blood between Wu and his father had caused Tony's death.

Tony was dead, and Jay would have to tell Louie. But there was something else, thought Jay. "I know." Wu's note had said. What did he know, Jay asked himself. He thought about Louie's words when Tony shot him. Could it be . . .? Jay ran downstairs and drove quickly to the hospital.

Chapter 14

Last wish

Louie was still in his hospital bed. Jay walked in and closed the door of his room.

"Father . . . I have some bad news," said Jay carefully. "Some very bad news."

Louie looked his son in the eye.

"Tony is dead," Jay said gently. "It was an accident. The police came in and saved me. Tony . . . the gun fired . . . it was a mistake."

Jay watched his father's face. Louie Kwan's face went gray. "Dead," he said.

"Yes," said Jay. "I'm sorry." He held his father's arm; it was something he hadn't done since he was a child.

Jay looked at his father; a single tear ran down his face. Jay hadn't seen his father cry since his mother had died.

"Father . . . I . . ."

"Tony, Tony . . ." said Louie Kwan softly. He lifted his hand to dry his face.

"Father," said Jay. "Is there something you want to tell me?"

"I . . . umm . . ."

"About Tony," said Jay. "When you were lying on the floor, you said 'my son.' But you weren't talking about me, were you?"

There was silence.

"Please," said Jay, "please tell me." He carefully took Tony's chain and pendant from his pocket and put them on Louie's bed.

Louie looked at them, and more tears fell from his eyes.

"Tell me, Father," Jay repeated, "tell me about Tony."

There was a long silence. Louie seemed to be thinking hard. Jay could hear the clock on the wall ticking. It seemed like hours. Then, finally, Louie spoke.

"Jessica Lee and I . . . we . . . as you know. Your mother didn't know, Kim Lee didn't know. Then Jessica had a baby . . ."

"Tony," said Jay.

"Yes," said Louie, "Tony." He turned his head away from Jay and into the pillows.

A few minutes later Louie sat up again. "But nobody knew that the child—Tony—was mine."

Jay waited.

"When Jessica was dying," Louie said, "she asked me not to tell anyone—ever. She said that it would bring shame on the Lee family."

The old man went on talking. "I couldn't tell anyone—not your mother, my family . . . or Tony. I felt so guilty about what I'd done, so bad. And your mother, I knew it would bring shame on her name, too, and shame on the Kwan family. How could I . . .? I couldn't do that. So I just . . ."

"You just . . . never told him!" Jay found it hard to believe.

"I kept him close to me," Louie went on, "I tried to protect him . . ."

"And you couldn't give him the restaurant . . ."

"Because if I had done that," Louie finished, "everyone would have known that he was a Kwan."

"You couldn't tell him that he was your son?" Jay said.

Louie put his head in his hands. Finally, he said, "I know I should have . . . but it was Jessica's dying wish. Her last wish. And I felt . . ."

"You lived with the secret," Jay said. "You let everyone believe that Tony was Kim Lee's son for all those years."

But it wasn't a complete secret. Jessica had told her sister. There was talk. Wu found out in jail from a friend of Jessica's sister, but he didn't tell Tony that he was Louie's son. He had saved that piece of information, thought Jay. He knew that when Tony killed Louie, Louie would know that he was being killed by his own son. That was the way he was going to pay Louie back for those fifteen years in jail!

Now Jay looked back at his father. He said, "Harry Wu wanted to kill you, and he found the cruelest way to do it."

And what happened was almost the worst thing that could happen, Jay thought. Tony was dead and Louie was in the hospital. The only good thing was that his father was alive, and Wu was going back to jail. It was just luck that his father wasn't dead, too.

"He never knew . . ." Louie cried, "he never knew!"

Jay tried to comfort his father. "You did what you thought was right," he said.

But his father could not be comforted. The old man turned his head into his pillows and cried.

Jay watched his father for a moment, still holding his arm. When he was a child he had thought that his father could never make a mistake. Now Jay was a man, and he saw that his father was also just a man. His father had made a big mistake in his life, and now he was paying for it.

Jay left his father's room. He stood at the window in the corridor. He thought about Tony—his half brother, the brother he never had. He thought about his father and how difficult he had been over the years. Perhaps Tony was part of the reason. Perhaps he was difficult because of that secret. Jay remembered something he had read somewhere: "Secrets are made to be found out with time." That was true, Jay thought. He shook his head. It was all so difficult to believe. But it was true.

He took his hands from his face and stood looking out of the window for a long time. The streets below were dark and here and there people were rushing home to their families. Jay thought about his father. It was going to take time for the two men to understand each other, and it wasn't going to be easy.

But in the end, he felt, it would be alright. It had to be alright.

Epilogue

Jay Kwan and his father walked into the graveyard next to the church. The young man held his father by the arm as they walked toward the new grave.

On the new gravestone was written: "Tony Lee-Kwan, son of Louie Kwan and Jessica Lee."

"It looks good," said Jay.

"Yes," said Louie. "It does."

"How's Micki getting on?" Jay asked. Micki Cheung was now the manager of The Golden Duck.

"He's good," said Louie, "a good manager."

"And . . . I want to tell you something," Louie continued.

"Yes?" said Jay, carefully.

Louie looked Jay in the eye.

"I want to tell you that I am happy that you are a private investigator," Louie went on. "You are very good."

Jay Kwan gave his father a gentle smile as he left him in the graveyard. Louie Kwan was a difficult man, but Jay now understood why. He loved his father just as he loved Chinatown. They both had their faults, but they were both part of his life. They were there, always in his life.

After all, thought Jay, home is home and blood is blood. He drove away through the dark, dirty streets of Chinatown.

Review: Chapters 1–4

A. Match the characters in the story with their descriptions.

1. Jay Kwan
2. Amy Trent
3. Louie Kwan
4. Ken Lau
5. Sonny Lo
6. Bernard Lom
7. Tony Lee
8. Milton Quon

a. a family friend

b. a famous Chinese-American artist.

c. an expert on handwriting

d. assistant private investigator

e. main chef at The Golden Duck

f. owner of Kwan's Investigation Agency

g. owner of the Jade Harbor

h. owner of The Golden Duck

B. Read each statement and circle whether it is true (T) or false (F).

1. Jay and his father have a very close relationship.   T / F

2. Jay would prefer to be a detective than manage a restaurant.   T / F

3. The fire in The Golden Duck started by accident.   T / F

4. Louie is a very respected chef.   T / F

5. Louie is happy that Jay is going to investigate the fire.   T / F

6. Bernard Lom is still angry with Louie Kwan.   T / F

7. Jay and Tony Lee grew up together.   T / F

C. Choose the best answer for each question.

1. When Louie says "blood is blood," what does blood represent?

   a. family

   b. blood

   c. health

   d. love

2. What is Amy implying in the following conversation?

   Amy: You have to be you.

   Jay: . . . but it's not so easy when you're the only son.

   Amy: Or daughter . . .

   a. She feels sorry for Jay.

   b. She knows it's difficult to be a son.

   c. She has felt pressure from her parents, too.

   d. It's easier to be a daughter.

D. Complete the crossword puzzle using the clues below.

Across

5. Louie says "Family is _____, blood is blood."

6. Bernard thinks Louie stole his _____.

10. Around Tony's neck, he wears a _____.

11. Jay's mother was an _____ _____.

12. Louie's restaurant is called The _____ _____.

13. Sonny Lo is an expert on _____.

Down

1. Bernard Lom's restaurant is The _____ _____.

2. Jay is an _____.

3. Bernard's restaurant has a good view of San Francisco _____.

4. Jay's grandfather was _____ Kwan.

7. Tony Lee is a _____.

8. One newspaper is the *San Francisco* _____.

9. What season is it in the story?

14. a kind of large Chinese pan

Review: Chapters 5–9

A. Number these events in the order in which they happened.

Jay goes to Tony's apartment. _____

Jay goes to The Red Door. _____

Jay hears an argument between his father and Tony Lee. _____

Jay and Amy go to The Golden Duck for dinner. _____

Jay meets Jackson in Union Square. _____

Jay drives to his father's house. _____

Tony hits Jay. _____

Jay and his father have an argument about managing The Golden Duck. _____

B. Choose the best answer for each question.

1. Where does Louie Kwan keep a gun?

   a. the kitchen of The Golden Duck

   b. his living room at home

   c. his bedroom at home

2. Why does Jay visit The Red Door?

   a. He wants a drink.

   b. He is looking for Harry Wu.

   c. He likes it.

3. When Harry Wu tells Jay that he's planning to live a quiet life, does Jay believe him?

    a. yes   b. no   c. He is not sure.

4. Why does Jay go back to The Golden Duck ?

    a. because he wants to fight with his father

    b. because Amy left her purse there

    c. because he wants to talk to Tony

5. Who does Jackson give Jay information about ?

    a. Harry Wu and Tony

    b. Harry Wu and a young Chinese chef

    c. Harry Wu and Louie

6. Why is Jay on the floor outside Tony's apartment ?

    a. because he feels ill

    b. because Tony has hit him

    c. because Tony ran into him

C. Write the place names in the puzzle. What is the hidden word? _____

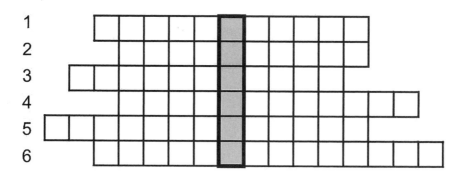

1. the place where Jackson and Jay meet (5 letters, 6 letters)

2. the bar where Jay meets Wu (3, 3, 4)

3. the café where Jackson sees Wu (3, 5, 3)

4. Tony's street (7, 5)

5. where Jay and Amy have dinner together (3, 6, 4)

6. part of San Francisco where Jay works (8, 6)

D. Answer each question.

1. What did Sonny Lo say about the writer of the note left in Louie's kitchen?

2. What does Jay ask Amy to do to Harry Wu?

3. What was "the young Chinese man" who Jackson saw talking to Harry Wu wearing?

4. What does Jay find on the floor near the door to Tony's apartment?

Review: Chapters 10–14

A. Read each statement and circle whether it is true (T) or false (F).

1. Tony believes that Louie killed his father.   T / F

2. Tony shoots Jay.   T / F

3. Louie tells Jay that he loved Jessica Lee.   T / F

4. Jay wants to get Harry Wu arrested.   T / F

5. Harry Wu made Tony shoot Louie.   T / F

6. Harry Wu tells Jay that Louie was Tony's father.   T / F

7. Jay tells his father that Tony is dead.   T / F

8. Louie says that he never told anyone that Tony was his son
   because Jessica Lee didn't want anyone to know.   T / F

9. In the end, Jay becomes manager of The Golden Duck.   T / F

B. Complete each sentence using the words in the box.

fake	brakes	controlling
record	evidence	coma

1. The police use an electronic device to _____ Harry Wu.

2. After being shot, Louie Kwan is in hospital, in a _____.

3. Harry Wu used a _____ police report to show Tony that Wu had
   killed his father.

4. The police report said that the _____ on the car hadn't worked.

5. The letters between Louie and Jessica were _____ that they
   loved each other.

6. Harry Wu is very _____: he likes to get others to commit
   crimes.

C. Choose the best answer for each question.

1. The story is called "Bad Blood" because _____.

   a. there is bad blood between Tony and Louie Kwan

   b. the bad blood between Harry Wu and Louie Kwan causes bad things to happen

   c. Jay hates his father

2. At the end of the story, Jay and his father _____.

   a. understand each other better

   b. realize that they will never understand each other

   c. hate each other

3. Choose the best summary of the theme of the book.

   a. It's difficult to keep a secret for a long time.

   b. Parents have got to let their children live their own lives.

   c. Children should try to understand their parents.

Answer Key

Chapters 1–4

A:

1. f; **2.** d; **3.** h; **4.** a; **5.** c; **6.** g; **7.** e; **8.** b

B:

1. F; **2.** T; **3.** F; **4.** T; **5.** F; **6.** F; **7.** T

C:

1. a; **2.** c

D:

1. Jade Harbor; **2.** investigator; **3.** bay; **4.** Winston; **5.** family;
6. recipe; **7.** chef; **8.** Chronicle; **9.** fall; **10.** pendant;
11. art teacher; **12.** Golden Duck; **13.** handwriting; **14.** wok

Chapters 5–9

A:

In order: 6, 2, 4, 3, 5, 8, 7, 1

B:

1. b; **2.** b; **3.** c; **4.** b; **5.** a; **6.** b

C:

1. Union Square; **2.** The Red Door; **3.** The Black Cat; **4.** Waverly Place;
5. The Golden Duck; **6.** Stockton Street

D:

1. The writer is controlling; **2.** to follow him, watch what he does and who
he talks to; **3.** a gold circle pendant; **4.** a note

Chapters 10–14

A:

1. T; **2.** F; **3.** T; **4.** T; **5.** T; **6.** F; **7.** T; **8.** T; **9.** F

B:
1. record; **2.** coma; **3.** fake; **4.** brakes; **5.** evidence; **6.** controlling

C:
1. b; **2.** a; **3.** Answers will vary.

Background Reading:

Family Relationships

A. Look at the information about Chinese parents in the survey and answer the questions below.

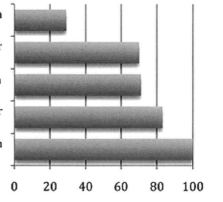

A Survey of Chinese Parents

29% of parents expect their children to become famous.

70% of parents want to send their children to study abroad.

71% of parents want their children to live a good life.

83% of parents want to send their children to the best schools.

100% of parents want their children to get the best education possible.

0   20   40   60   80   100

1. Do the results of this survey surprise you?

2. Do you think the results would be the same in your country?

B. One main theme of *Bad Blood* is the relationship between Jay and his father. Read about a famous father and child, and answer the questions that follow.

Father and daughter: Bruce and Shannon Lee

Bruce Lee
actor, martial artist, director, writer

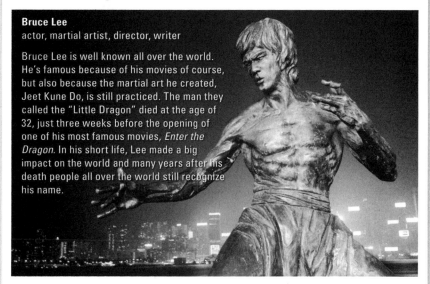

Bruce Lee is well known all over the world. He's famous because of his movies of course, but also because the martial art he created, Jeet Kune Do, is still practiced. The man they called the "Little Dragon" died at the age of 32, just three weeks before the opening of one of his most famous movies, *Enter the Dragon*. In his short life, Lee made a big impact on the world and many years after his death people all over the world still recognize his name.

**Shannon Emery Lee-Keasler
(Lee Heung Yee)**
actress

Bruce Lee's daughter, Shannon Lee, was only four years old when her father died, but she still thinks about him often. "His death still affects me daily," she says, "in the sense that I wish for what I don't have." Shannon says that other people expect her to be a fighter, like her father. But, she says: "I'm not really like him . . . I'm definitely the lazy one in the family. My dad and my brother Brandon were a lot more active." Shannon Lee has acted in some martial arts movies. She also runs the Bruce Lee Foundation, an organization that preserves the martial arts and philosophy of Bruce Lee.

1. Do you think that Bruce Lee would be disappointed that Shannon didn't become a fighter, like him?

2. Do you think that the relationship between son/daughter and parent is different when the parent is famous? Why? Why not?

Background Reading:

San Francisco's Chinatown

A. Read at the information about San Francisco's Chinatown and match the places or events in the passage to the pictures on page 91.

Thinking of visiting San Francisco's Chinatown?

Chinatown begins at the famous Chinatown Gate (1) at Grant Avenue and Bush Street. This gate was a gift from the Republic of China in 1969. San Francisco's oldest street—Grant Avenue—runs eight blocks through the center of Chinatown, home to the largest Chinese population outside Asia.

Don't miss the open markets (2) on Stockton Street, which sell everything you could want from clothes and toys, to fruits and vegetables, fish and meats. You can also visit the little alleys between Grant and Stockton, which are full of restaurants with their food on display (3). These are some of the most interesting parts of Chinatown!

The best way to explore San Francisco's Chinatown is by just walking through the streets. The best time to visit is in January and February, when Chinatown is decorated in bright colors and people gather to watch the dragon dances (4) and parades in celebration of Chinese New Year.

Bring your walking shoes and be prepared to take back lots of gifts and a full stomach!

B. Answer the questions below.

1. Which parts of San Francisco's Chinatown do you think you'd like to visit?

2. Do you know of other cities that have a Chinatown?

Background Reading:

Spotlight on . . .

Private Investigators

A. Read the information about being a private investigator and answer the questions below.

Facts and figures: Being a private investigator

- Work hours are often irregular, and the work can be dangerous.

- Investigators generally work alone.

- About 30% of private investigators are self-employed.

- Investigators typically have related experience in areas such as law, insurance, the military, government, or intelligence jobs.

- A lot of a private investigator's work is done using a computer.

- There are about 60,000 private investigators working in the USA.

- Average investigators earn between $24,000 and $58,000 a year.

- About 15% of private investigators are women.

Adapted from U.S. Department of Labor Bureau of Labor Statistics (www.bls.gov)

---

1. Do any of these facts about private investigators surprise you?

2. Would you be interested in being a private investigator? Why? Why not?

B. **What type of person makes a successful private investigator? Put the personal qualities in order from most important (1) to least important (7).**

_____ curiosity

_____ ability to write well

_____ creativity

_____ wide life experience

_____ love of facts

_____ patience

_____ ability to communicate

C. **Read the interview and see if the writer agrees with your order in B.**

What do you need to be a good private investigator?

I would say that any successful detective must first have the ability to communicate. This means that he or she must have the ability to connect with people of all walks of life. It also means that the investigator must have the ability to clearly present a simple fact or a complex investigation in writing. The end result of an investigation is the report, which is given to the client upon conclusion of the assignment. You have to be able to write well. Patience is very important, too, partly because private investigators spend a lot of time waiting.

Also, we are in the business of providing facts, not opinions; we let our clients draw their own conclusions from our report, so great investigators have to love facts. Then come creativity and curiosity, both important qualities. Lastly, I believe that every investigator should possess varied life experience.

Glossary

accident   (*n.*)   something unpleasant that happens to someone and that was not intended, sometimes causing injury or death

alley   (*n.*)   a narrow passage or street with buildings or walls on both sides

chef   (*n.*)   a cook in a restaurant or hotel

coma   (*n.*)   a state of deep unconsciousness

enemy   (*n.*)   someone who hates you or wants to harm you

evidence   (*n.*)   anything you see, experience, read, or are told that causes you to believe something is true or has really happened

fake   (*adj.*)   made to look valuable or genuine, usually in order to deceive people

forgery   (*n.*)   the crime of forging money, documents, or paintings

grave   (*n.*)   a place where a dead person is buried

jukebox   (*n.*)   a coin-operated machine that plays music

mistake   (*n.*)   something that you did not intend to do, or that produces a result you did not want

overalls   (*n.*)   pants attached to a piece of cloth that covers the chest and has two straps going over the shoulders

parole   (*n.*)   the time when a prisoner is released before the official end of their prison sentence and has to promise to behave well

pendant   (*n.*)   an ornament or piece of jewelry on a chain that you wear around your neck

stubborn   (*adj.*)   determined to do what one wants and unwilling to change one's mind